SIMPLIFYING FINANCE AND ACCOUNTING (F&A) FUNCTION

(A PRACTICAL APPROACH FOR FINANCE AND ACCOUNTS IN AN ORGANISATION)

BY: DAUJI GUPTA

A Useful Notebook for Business Managers and Fresher Financial Professionals and Student to have practical exposure in finance and accounts.

SIMPLIFYING FINANCE AND ACCOUNTING (F&A) FUNCTION (A PRACTICAL APPROACH)

ACKNOWLEDGEMENTS

I am thankful to all my Gurus (teachers) and colleagues in past as well as in present who supported / guided through my career and provided me platform to enhance my skills at all times. Also, I would like to thank my parents and extended family for valuable support to made me strong and enthusiastic for writing this book.

- *Dauji Gupta*

NOTE ABOUT THE BOOK

Finance & Accounting (F&A) function is generally everywhere in every business, without finance one cannot think to even start a business. Therefore, Need of **FINANCE** to start / run a business and Need of **ACCOUNTING** for better control ship on every stage of business is must for every business.

Better Management of F&A function lead to organisation to successful organisation. In General, especially in small/medium size organizations, F&A team is also regulated by business owners / CEO who have limited knowledge of F&A team and due to which some of important aspects in F&A team is missed out and that may result in losses or lesser returns in business.

To compete with such requirement, this book is being drafted to compile all aspects of F&A team in every business together at one place to make reader more knowledgeable with F&A function in short and crisp manner. It contains the ways to manage Finance and Accounting function (F&A) in a smart and better way in every organisation. This is being prepared with professional knowledge and acquired experience of market carries with the writer. Although, this book contents F&A related information, which generally a finance professional knows very well, and may be better than this, but idea to write this book to consolidate all areas at one place and to provide platform to new-comers/ non-finance people to understand F&A function and value thereof in business.

This book is planned with below objectives:

- ✓ To stream line F&A function of an organisation, especially start-ups.
- ✓ To prepare SOPs of an organisation's F&A function for better management to results optimization of profitability.
- ✓ To provide platform to fresher finance professionals to learn about their organisational responsibilities
- ✓ To enhance knowledge of Non-Finance people (CEO/ Business managers) of Organisation to know the F&A role and areas where F&A function can support to business

This book is not containing the technical knowledge of finance and accounting as it always with finance professionals, rather this book contains answers about questions such as, what are the areas look into by F&A people in an organization? How and when to use various F&A tactics? And also, some knowledge about key F&A Terms.

This is an attempt to accumulate major F&A tactics at one place in simple language so that user can understand easily, however one may have different view.

CONTENTS

INTRODUCTION

Further to explain, F&A function involve in each and every area of business process starting from Product Development to Payments. Please refer below chart to get clarity of F&A role in business process:

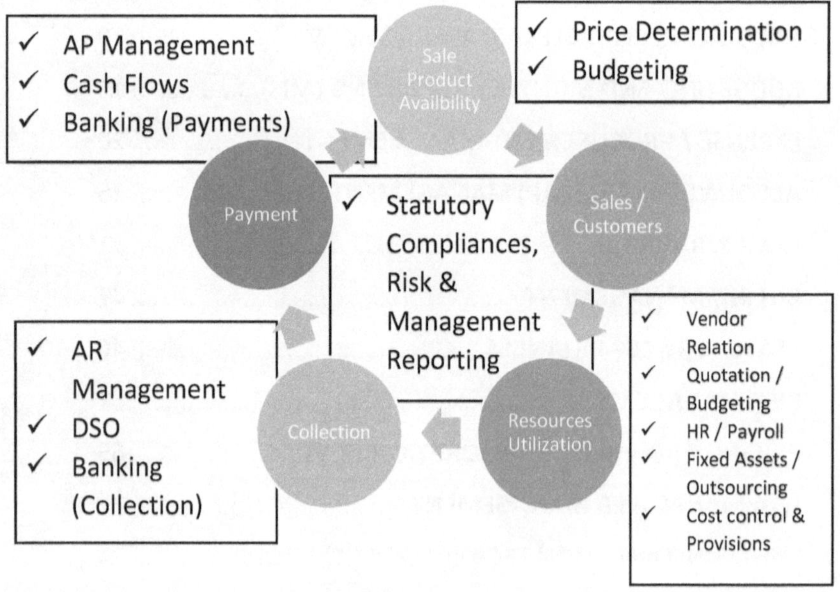

Hence, this book is drafted to capture each and every aspect of various parts involve in F&A function of an organisation, as listed down below and we have separate chapter for every part below and last chapter with summarization of all F&A function:

A. Account Receivable (AR)

B. Budgeting and Monthly Reporting (MIS)

C. Expense / Procurement Management

D. Account Payable (AP)

E. Cash and Banking

F. Billing Process / Management

G. Statutory Compliances

H. Risk Management

I. Pricing / Relevant & Absorption Costing (a guidance to sales)

J. F&A Manpower Management

K. Use of Information Technology (IT) tools

ACCOUNT RECEIVABLE (AR) MANAGEMENT

Account Receivable Management is key area of F&A in every organisation role, where starting from "Interaction to Customer" to "Timely Collection from Customer" with objective of satisfied customers with best services. So before starting role of F&A, lets list down activities involve in AR management, such as:

✓ Getting Leads of Customer and approach to customer

✓ Sales Proposal to Customer

✓ Customer Acceptance of Proposal / Introduction of customer to organisation

✓ Master Creation / Documentation of customer before start services / Sale

✓ Services / Sales rendering to customers and Billing

✓ Billing Submission and Automated outstanding follow-ups

✓ Collections

✓ Customer Feedback and re-sales

With reference to listed down above activities, F&A function needs to establish necessary controls in almost each above area. And that can be promulgated within organisation by way of full-fledge Customer/Credit Management policy covering below aspects:

- ✓ Providing Inputs about customer leads to Sales people, such as from Newspaper, MCA website competitor's data, Business magazines etc. This gives extra strength to sales.
- ✓ Sales Proposal Cost-benefit Analysis and Legal check in case of agreements
- ✓ Customer Documentation & Master Creation:
  - o Know your customer (KYC) Form having a standardised Format with necessary details as per business requirements, to be taken from customer's authorised person with sign / stamp along with relevant supporting documents
  - o Credit Request Form (CRF) having a standardised format with customer request for credit (Amount / period / Interest applicability) and jointly agreed by sales person with mentioning sales proposal / rates.
  - o Verification of documents and creation of Master in system and filing of same documents for future purpose.

✓ Billing to customers with Maker-checker concept based on sales proposal and meeting Tax compliances (Presently GST applicable in India)

✓ Outstanding Follow-ups based on various reports such as:
- o Debtors Ageing Report being: (as per business requirements)
  - Segment Wise (like Service A, B, C etc)
  - Sales Person wise
  - Categories defining
  - E.g.: Red Zone, Orange Zone, Green Zone, Black Zone
    - o Red – Customers having Old Dues no present dues
    - o Orange – Customers having Old & Present both dues
    - o Green Zone – Customer having present dues
    - o Black Zone – Customer with Legal Cases
  - This will help to reader in prioritising customers for following up for collection
- o DSO Calculation and Trending along with relevant Debtors ageing report.

- o DSO (Daily Sales Outstanding) also referred as Debtors turnover ratio, tells the reader AR is having how much days sales and looking with trend with segment wise, reader can know which area is improving and which is requiring more attention of the team.

- o Periodic Balance Confirmation Letters/Emails to All customer except some exceptions as per business requirements. May be Quarterly or half yearly depend upon business requirement. This will help organization to know about billing gaps, billing submission gaps, customer disputes, and plus a good follow-up practice.

✓ Collection

- o by Cheques – Use of CMS services from Bank for better accounting and control.

- o By PDC Cheques – Declaration letter along with PDC for non-failure of cheques.

- o E-collections - Communication of Proper Bank Details to customer and giving preference for e-modes.

- o Bill of exchanges / Letter of Credit (LC) – Proper documentations and controls.

- o   Timely accounting of same to have better control on reporting, further follow-up for rest dues and customer satisfaction.

✓ Reporting after sales and collections:

- o   Evaluation of customer profitability report / Segment profitability

- o   Decision to change in pricing / discount with objective to increase business.

- o   Customer Feedback for determining betterment of services.

*****

Key Documents – Customer / Credit Management Policy, Debtors Reports Formats

BUDGETING AND MONTHLY REPORTING (MIS)

This is also one of important area of F&A function which helps in controlling overall business structure, in terms of Sales, Costs, Cash-flows, Statutory Compliances and manpower efficiency & performance.

Budgeting, also referred as **Forecasting,** starts before start of financial year, where F&A team projects for next financial year for sales, expenses, cash flows and overall financial position keeping base of previous year and planned new business activities. For starts-up, this is like platform to be settled-up for future course of actions in business. Budgeting also helps in delegating of powers for routine matters in business, i.e., budgeted items, such as approval for expenses, investment etc.

After finish budgeting, monthly reporting system, known as **Management Information System (MIS)** comes into picture. In MIS, every month actual position of overall business, is being presented to management along with 1) comparison of budgets & previous period data, 2) analysis thereof and 3) other useful information happened in the particular period.

MIS structure is defined based on business requirement covering all aspects of business, such as, Operations Numbers, Segment-wise Revenue, Costs, Manpower, working capital, Cash flows, Assets, investment, compliances etc. so that gap can be identified easily at maximum micro level and control can be established in case anything is not meeting up with the desired results.

In small organisation or organisation where monthly review is not possible, Quarterly Statement are preferred in place of monthly one.

Overall objective of Budgeting and MIS is to control over business in form of identifying gaps and taking corrective actions immediately so that problem is resolved at inception itself otherwise difficulties may arise at year end to cover large gaps. Now we need to discuss detailed requirement in Budgeting and MIS statements.

<u>Budgeting</u> – Please note below points kept in mind at the time of budgeting:

- ✓ Detailing of previous year/base year figure should be summarised in well manner for Revenue, Expenses, Assets, compliances etc.
- ✓ In case of new company First year, figures need to be planned after considering all possible factors and discussion with Middle and Top management.
- ✓ Figures are to be differentiate within months since business cannot remain as it is every month across year. E.g. Near Diwali, Staff welfare/ Business promotion expenses are more, so budgeting for such expenses should be extra in those months.
- ✓ Budget should comprise of below projections:
    - o Business Numbers (Quantum)
    - o Revenue / Discount at deep level
    - o Direct & Indirect Expenses
    - o Manpower and Staff Costs
    - o Capital Expenditure
    - o Statutory Compliances
    - o Working Capital and Cash Flows
    - o Overall Financial Summary Projection
    - o Any other information as per business requirement

<u>**MIS**</u> – A MIS of any organisation should represent below information for management:

- ✓ Comparison with Budgets
- ✓ Comparison with same period previous year
- ✓ MIS should be presented by 5th- 10th Day of following month (Quarterly MIS by 15th-20th day of following month)
- ✓ MIS should contain below data / and analysis thereof:
    - o Business Numbers at deep level
    - o Revenue and Direct expenses at deep level
    - o Indirect Expenses
    - o Manpower Numbers & Its Expenses
    - o Status of Working Capital – Debtors, Creditors & others
    - o Cash Flows
    - o Financial Summary
    - o Statutory Compliance Status
    - o List of expiring agreements in next 2 months along with status of follow-ups
    - o Any other information as per business requirement
- ✓ MIS review is also must to have control on overall business in terms of:
    - o Analysis of Deviation from budget
    - o Analysis of deviation from previous period figures
    - o Comparison of profitability / ROCE among business segments
    - o Other analysis of financial position of organisation.

*****

Key Documents – Budget Documents / Format, MIS Formats

SIMPLIFYING F&A FUNCTION BY DAUJI GUPTA [19]

EXPENSE / PROCUREMENT MANAGEMENT

In expense management, objective is to have best resources at best prices by having full fledge process in place in organisation to meet timelines and efficiency requirement.

For Managing expenses/ procurement in an organisation, F&A needs to divide expenses in below category:
- ✓ Capital Expenditure
- ✓ Direct Expenses
- ✓ Indirect Expenses
- ✓ Staff related Expenses
- ✓ Statutory Expenses/ Taxes

For above listed categories, organisation should have Delegation of Authority (DOA) policy in place to decide who can approve these expenses/ Vendor Invoices for processing for payment. DOA Policy basically contains below:

- ✓ Limits up to which certain managers/officers can approve Budgeted expenses
- ✓ Limits up to which certain managers/officers can approve Non-Budgeted expenses
- ✓ Procedure to selection of any vendor
- ✓ Need of Purchase order and issuance of same
- ✓ Procedure to Process any vendor invoices (Disbursement Checklist)
- ✓ Any other useful information as per business requirement.

With reference to DOA and Expenses management below points to be kept in mind for each category of payment:

Capital Expenditure:

✓ Float enquiry with at least 2-4 vendors to get quotations to compare quality and costs.

✓ In case of small capex items, quotation may be limited to two and for higher amounts, it can be asked for 3-4 vendor quotations.

✓ Standardised capital Expenditure Form to be filled by user and present before management for process along with quotations and comparisons.

✓ Limits should be defined for expenses, who can approve how much expenses for what type of expenses.

✓ Big Capital Expenditure, like projects, new unit / factory setup etc, which are being planned for earning returns, are being analysed with tools provided with concept called **"CAPITAL BUDGETING"**. Capital Budgeting, basically, refers to compare cost and returns between several alternative based on best suitable option. There are several options to analysis such proposals, popular are IRR & NPV as explained below:

o IRR (Internal Rate of return) – which provides expected return on project considering investment / loan/ interest and cash inflows (income/cost or tax benefits) etc.

o NPV (Net Present Value) – It provides the present value of options after considering discounting factors for future inflow and outflows from the investment. (Note: cost saving is cash inflow)

Direct Expenditure:

✓ In case of Routine expenses and expenses being reimbursed by customer, Approval limits can be liberalised or make in line with customers agreed terms.

✓ Expenses having higher amounts being reimbursed by customers should be paid after receipt of advance from customer or approval from top management if own funds to be used.

✓ In case of expenses being nature of Optional Service Provider, it's a good practice to have at least 2-3 vendors in panel and have review of rates periodically, say annually, to maintain cost controls with efficiency and quality. Such as Transporter, Direct Material provider etc.

✓ Expenses, of being non-routine and even agreed by customers to reimburse or not, approval should be aggressive to include top management, such as penalties, delay service, or double use of service etc.

Indirect Expenditure:

✓ Here limits can be liberalised for budgeted expenses and for non-budgeted expenses, limits should be restricted with top management.
✓ Quotation should be asked from 2-3 vendors depend of size of expenses (whole contract*), say:
  o Upton INR 10,000 – No Quotation
  o INR 10001 to – INR 50,000 – 2 Quotation
  o Above INR 50,000 – 3 Quotation

  (if contract is INR 5000 per month for a year, Contract amount is INR 60,000 and 3 quotation should be received, in line with above limits)*

✓ Please note below keys points for possible categories of expenses:
  o **Advertising / Sales Promotion** – Limits should be with Sales Head
  o **Office Rent / Utilities** – Budgeted expenses can be with Finance Manager and non-budgeted ones with top management.
  o **Legal & professional** - Budgeted expenses can be with Finance Manager and non-budgeted ones with top management.
  o **Other Administrative/ office expenses** – Budgeted expenses can be with Finance Manager and non-budgeted ones with top management.
  o **Interest & Finance Expenses** – should be approved by Top Management / Board of

Directors. *(Ideally an organisation should have at least 2 bankers/ finance – institution tie ups for Loans/finance limits, if application to maintain proper negotiation)*

- o **Profit / Loss on sale of Assets** – Limits should be with top management.
- o **Writing off / Bad debts** – should be as per Credit / Customer Management policy as defined in Chapter A.
- o **Conveyance / Travelling / Mobile Bill / or other employees related expenses** – there should be some HR policy with having limits for various designation and procedure for payment. A good HR/Employee policy should have:
  - Recruitment and reallocation related procedure
  - Working Hours / Leave policy
  - Salary Increment/ Performance Appraisal Procedure
  - Conveyance & travelling
  - Medical Insurance / Heath Benefit expenses
  - Mobile Phone
  - Welfare related activities
  - Code of Conduct and Other statutory policies
- o **Statutory Payments** – with Finance Managers

*****

Key Documents – Delegation of Authority (DOA) Policy

ACCOUNT PAYABLE (AP) MANAGEMENT

Accounts payable management is being extension of Expenses Management. Once expense is incurred/managed / controlled, AP management comes into picture.

Accounts payable management is being exercise of:

- ✓ To have complete expense accounting/provision for the given period
- ✓ To have limited dues with statutory vendors
- ✓ To have timely payment for having satisfied vendors
- ✓ To have corrected disbursement and accounting
- ✓ To have defined and professional mechanism to manage vendors etc

Hence, with reference to achieve above mentioned objective, F&A needs to be have below controls at various stage of interaction with vendors:

Initial stage of Supply/Service:

- ✓ Collection of KYC documents of Finalized vendors and verification of same to avoid unwanted vendors; such as: (In India - PAN/COI/GSTIN/TRADE LICENSE/IEC etc.)
- ✓ Issuance of Purchase order and acceptance from vendors on same including defined terms and conditions to avoid future dispute.

✓ Define Payment Term in purchase order itself.
✓ To have Legal Agreement in case contract is in nature of Long term, say period of 1 year or more or involve high costs.
✓ Review of Rates at the time of renewal of agreements.

At stage of Supply/Service:

✓ Issue of receipt of Goods and service whether in physical form or by emails etc
✓ Mentioning of any discrepancy, if any, at the time of acceptance of service (by User).
✓ Receipt of invoices by organisation along with remark of receipt date
✓ Submission of invoice to accounts

After Service

✓ Compilation of all documents as per Disbursement Checklist**
*(**F&A team should have Disbursement checklist for account user to compile all documents together and file and processing for payment. Disbursement checklist may include list of documents and approval required for processing payment for different kind of expenses as per business requirement.)*
✓ Accounting of all expenses and ensuring necessary approvals in place as per DOA.

- ✓ Ensuring for statutory compliances such as GST, TDS, ESI etc (in India).
- ✓ Proceeding for Payment with proper channel on due dates. And give preference to E-modes of payment.
- ✓ Obtain receipt of payment from vendor.

Other than above controls at various stages, F&A team should be reporting in MIS on accounts payable to manage vendor payments more efficiently and same can be list down as follows:

- ✓ Payables in ageing form along with MIS in different segments
- ✓ Highlighting disputes cases to management for older dues or non-account dues along with reasons thereof
- ✓ Proper detailing of non-accounted dues into provisions to have matching principle in place. Similarly, for prepaid expenses.
- ✓ Highlighting risk of non-payment to certain vendors, such as 1) Non-payment to registered small scale industry vendor may results in paying of Interest, 2) non-payment to vendor in specified period may cost statutory compliance, e.g. In India, where GST credit have been taken in books, may require to pay GST after 6 months of non-payment to vendor; etc.
- ✓ Separate List of Statutory dues along with due interest and penalty till date to be presented.
- ✓ Dispute cases to be referred to legal department

- ✓ Status of Imprest/Advance accounts with employees and accounting thereof
- ✓ Any other information as per business requirements.

As a good accounting practice, F&A needs to collect periodic Balance confirmation / No Dues letter from vendors. It should Quarterly/Half yearly/Annually as per business requirement. One standard No Dues letter should be kept by F&A team to send to vendors as and when required.

*****

Key Documents – Disbursement Checklist, Accounts Payable Report Format, No Dues letter format.

CASH & BANKING

Cash and Bank handling is the task to be handled/controlled/supervised by experienced and trusted people in the organisation. While handling cash/banking, a due care is needed at every step, since error of 1 digit can results in unwanted costs to company. Ideally cash transactions should be minimized to possible extent.

Here, we will list out control / procedure required for cash and banking separately as per below.

CASH RECEIPTS

Due to unavoidable reason of receipt through Banking mode, organisation, in some cases, needs to accept cash from customers. Other minor receipts from imprest/advance return from employee etc are not discussed here. So, with reference to receipts, below points needs to be noted:

- ✓ Instead of receipt from customers, we can ask customers to deposit cash directly in organisation bank account in possible cases and ask customer to send deposit slips via email or with letter.
- ✓ Other than small receipts, (Says More than INR 10,000), organisation should insist customer to give letter stating payment in cash against due invoices on its letterhead with sign and stamp.
- ✓ Each receipt should be accounted at instantly and receipt to be issued to customer instantly.

✓ Receipts at the day end, should be counted and tallied with accounts and arrangement needs to be done to deposit cash next day in bank along with proper accounting.

✓ In case cash needed for payment also, that can be used from receipts funds. However ideally received cash should be deposited in bank next day to control fake/stale currency, especially where cash received is more from one/two customer.

CASH PAYMENTS

Cash payments are generally required for routine office expenses. However, in general case, cash payment to vendors to be restricted to maximum possible extent. With reference to payments, below points needs to be noted:

✓ Every cash Payment needs to account first and receipt from Payee needs to be taken on voucher itself.

✓ In case of accounting is not possible at same time, printed form of cash voucher is being used to mention details in same, along with approval and bills and then receipt from payee is taken on same.

✓ Cash payment should be in line with statutory norms, like, India:
   ○ Cash payment should not be excess of INR 10,000 to single party in single day.

- At the time of payment of more than INR 5000, Receipt from Payee needs to be taken on Revenue Stamp of Re.1/- (Stamp Duty rules) (i.e., Signature of Payee on voucher after affixing revenue stamp on same), etc.

BANKING

Banking is also an important area of F&A, which virtually manages all type of report to maintain their correctness level. Also, in present era, Banks provides various facilities in terms of online banking, functioning, reporting etc. so it is also good to have maximum of such banking services, some of same are listed below for reference:

- ✓ Online Payments by e-transfer/NEFT /RTGS
- ✓ Online requests for printing of cheques/Demand Drafts
- ✓ Online Trade net banking to process foreign payments / Bank Guarantees/ Letter of credits etc.
- ✓ Sweep in Facilities between intra company bank accounts including automatization of Fixed deposits / Credit to Cash Credit Accounts
- ✓ CMS (Cash Management Services) from bank:
  - To Get delivery of printed cheques/DD without going bank

- o To deposit cash/Cheques in bank without getting bank along with automatic e-reports of same.
- ✓ Email/ Fax Indemnity activation with bank for acceptance of documents over email by bank for urgent cases.

COLLECTIONS

- ✓ In case of collections, accounting entry should be processed:
  - o For collected cheques, on same day before depositing cheques into bank
  - o For E-collections, on next day for collected dues in previous day by taking extracts of bank statement of previous day.
- ✓ For cheque collections; Users (Who collecting cheques from customers) to be trained to ensure below points in cheques:
  - o No Overwriting on cheques
  - o Correct name of organisation as drawee name in cheque
  - o No future date
  - o No past date more than 3 months
  - o Amount in word matches with Amount in figures
  - o Drawer Signature at proper place in cheque
  - o Mention customer name on back of cheque if different drawer (e.g., proprietorship firms, DD/Pay-order etc)

- ✓ Post-dated cheques (PDC) to be accompanied with No-Failure Declaration letter from Customer. (A standard letter format to be prepared as per business requirement)
- ✓ Forex Receipts should be accounted as per FIRC/Bank Advice received from customer, where charges from overseas bank needs to be accounted carefully. *(Negotiation from Banks is required to have minimum costs in Forex receipt and payment based on defined margin over Inter-bank rate (IBR))*
- ✓ Other Points may be defined as per business requirement.

PAYMENTS

- ✓ Minimization of payment by cheques or rather minimization of hand-written cheques.
- ✓ While paying by cheques, below points needs to be kept in mind:
  - o Payment entry should be in place before printing cheque
  - o No Overwriting on cheques
  - o Correct name of vendor as drawee name in cheque
  - o Amount in word matches with Amount in figures
  - o Authorised Signature at proper place in cheque as per Board Resolution
  - o Account Payee Cheques

- ✓ While paying by E-modes (NEFT/RTGS/e-transfer), below points needs to be noted:
    - o Cancelled cheque or certified bank details from vendors' bank should be obtained
    - o From Cancelled cheque / received Bank details, below needs to be verified:
        - ▪ Drawee Name
        - ▪ Bank Account No.
        - ▪ IFS Code
    - o Before payment, Payment entry should be in place and should be kept before authorised signatory along with relevant bills and vouchers for verification.
    - o In cases, Payee name is different from vendor name as appearing on invoices, a declaration should be obtained on vendor letter head regarding reasons thereof, mostly in case of proprietorship firm.
- ✓ Authorised signatories should be trained to verify payment amount with invoice amount.
- ✓ To avoid duplicity of payment against same invoice, below procedure should be implemented:
    - o Payment preference on basis of Original Invoices along with Accounting of purchase/service/expense voucher with necessary approvals as per DOA.
    - o Accounting voucher should have vendor invoice same as appearing on invoice, no differentiation

should be allowed (even for Space/Dot/Comma etc) (Since most of accounting software control duplicate invoice accounting of same vendor)
- o Putting Paid Stamp on invoices at the time of payment with date of payment. And initials on same by Authorised signatory at time of payment approval/cheque signing.

BANK RECONCILIATION STATEMENTS (BRS)

BRS known as back bone of accounting of banking transactions. Unless you have BRS, you cannot be sure about correctness of banking transaction in books, which affect almost all kind of report being used by management in routine business. Ideally BRS should be prepared on daily/twice a day, however in small organisation it can be relaxed to Weekly basis. BRS represents below 4 type of differences:

1. Cheques/Payment issued but not cleared in Bank
2. Cheques/Payment debited in bank but not accounted in books
3. Collections accounted in books but not cleared in Bank
4. Collections received in Bank but not accounted

For having controlled over BRS, below points should be noted in each category:

1. Cheques/Payment issued but not cleared in Bank

- ✓ Anything older than 5-7 days in this category, to be reviewed whether its correct or some other cause of being reflecting here. (e.g. if payment is done by NEFT and at the time of entry into bank website, due to wrong details, payment might not happen),
- ✓ In case cases, there might be chances due to difference in amount accounted and amount actually debited in bank account and same needs to reconciled with point 2 cases. (E.g. Entry of INR 3283/- and payment 3823/-)
- ✓ Entry Payment should not be older than 3 months in any case, if so, those payment to be reverse immediately and creditor to be re-stood to correct amount.

2. Cheques/Payment debited in bank but not accounted in books

- ✓ There may be instances where debit comes from bank and needs to be account by accounts department, such cases can be reported here.
- ✓ Ideally there should not be any entry in this category older than 2-3 days as it shows poor accounting.
- ✓ Cases like payment without entry, double payment against single account entry, different debit from accounted entry amount, Dishonour of cheque

collected etc being coming here and same needs to be rectified on immediate basis.

3. Collections accounted in books but not cleared in Bank

✓ There are some cases which represents cheque deposited in bank and under clearing with bank.

✓ Ideally there should not be any entry in this category older than 4-5 days as it shows somewhere gap in depositing the cheque into bank, cheque return from bank due to short mistakes etc. and such gaps needs to controlled and minimized.

✓ Cases like entry without deposit in bank, double entry against single cheque collected, different Credit from accounted entry amount etc being coming here and same needs to be rectified on immediate basis.

4. Collections received in Bank but not accounted

✓ There are some cases which represents collections deposited in bank, like NEFT/RTGS received and pending for accounting.

✓ There are some cases, where funds received in bank account and does not accounted in books due to pending information from Bank/Sales& ops Team about customer name. and the same should be asked to Bank on immediate basis to account the same (since bank can provide payer name for every transaction credited in bank account).

- ✓ Ideally there should not be any entry in this category older than 2-3 days as it shows somewhere gap in accounting entry of collected cheques, accounting with different amount etc. and such gaps needs to controlled and minimized.
- ✓ Cases like entry without deposit in bank, double entry against single cheque collected, different Credit from accounted entry amount etc being coming here and same needs to be rectified on immediate basis.

Reporting with MIS

- ✓ Funds Flows summary
- ✓ Loan Accounts Report with due EMI in next month
- ✓ Weekly Fund flow requirement/Planning
- ✓ Clean BRS on month end
- ✓ Status of Imprest Accounts

*****

Key Documents – PDC Letter, BRS Format, Funds Flows Report.

BILLING MANAGEMENT

Billing is the back bone of a business, which is first step to receipt money from customers for Goods/services supplied to them, where it is required to have at least below:

- ✓ Corrected Billing
- ✓ Timeline-ness
- ✓ Tax complied
- ✓ Legal complied

To achieve this, organisation should have below:

INVOICE FORMAT

- ✓ Party Name, Address, Date, Account head, Description, quantity, rate, currency, Amount, Tax etc.
- ✓ Due Date
- ✓ Tax Complied (Presently GST in India), like HSN/SAC, Place of supply, Export/SEZ etc.
- ✓ Amount in figures and Amount in words
- ✓ Tax Amount clarity.
- ✓ Necessary declaration / service details
- ✓ Maker – Checker concept (Bill preparation by A and approved by B – as per DOA)
- ✓ Authorised person signature / Digital Signature
- ✓ Proper Bank Details (Nostro account details in case of overseas billing)
- ✓ Terms & Conditions

TERMS & CONDITIONS

There should be always mentioning of terms and conditions on each invoice printed to have most legal complied invoice; such as:

- ✓ Clause for acceptance of Errors and Omission
- ✓ Acceptance of Disputes if informed within requisite days
- ✓ Interest in case of payment delay than due date @certain rate.
- ✓ Other clauses as per business requirement

PRE-BILLING

There should be Pre-billing checklist containing information for billing user to bill to customer. And same should be prepared by Ops / Sales team in a standard format to capture all required details as desired by F&A team. Pre-billing should contain:

- ✓ Type of Goods/Services supplied
- ✓ Rates whether Standard / Specific. In case specific, either rates to be mentioned or reference approval to be mentioned.
  (Specific/Special rates approval to be taken in line with DOA/Customer Policy in place)

- ✓ Type of Extra Goods/services provided than agreed terms
- ✓ Extra Re-imbursement to be billed
- ✓ Any other useful information deemed to communicate to billing user (Depends upon business requirement)

BILLING SUBMISSION

- ✓ Bill needs to be submitted to customer within 2-3 days.
- ✓ It's always a good practice to send invoice by Email in present era.
- ✓ While invoice is being sent by email, "a non-required-signature clause" to be mentioned on same.
- ✓ If invoice send by courier, then a register to be maintained where POD should be captured.
- ✓ In case of hand delivery, a proper receipt of invoices to be documented to avoid future disputes.
- ✓ In Nutshell, a billing submission register can be maintained either in E-form or physical form depending upon business requirement.

*****

Key Documents – Invoice Format, Pre-billing check List, Bill Submission Register.

STATUTORY COMPLIANCES

In an organisation, there are various statutory compliances involve in terms of Constitution related, Business Requirement, Labour and Industrial Related, Direct Taxes, Indirect Taxes etc.

Generally, most of compliances are managed by F&A team in most of organisations. To manage various applicable statutory compliances in present era with reference to business requirement, it is necessary to have a control sheet by F&A team for such compliances. And needs to be presented to management with MIS for every month and in case any thing pending for previous month that should be also included in same.

This control sheet can be termed as **Statutory Compliance Chart** and should include below:

✓ Name of Statutory Compliance (type of tax/license etc)
✓ Activity (Renewal, Tax payment, Return filing etc)
✓ Applicable period (Month, Quarter, Year etc)
✓ Due date
✓ Status / Completion date
✓ Delay, if any
✓ Penalty/ interest on delay till date, if any
✓ Other remarks

Whereas if we compile first 3 field in a document, that can be also termed as **Tax Calendar** for the organisation.

STATUTORY COMPLIANCES APPLICABLE IN INDIA (CY 2018)

We will discuss here important ones in each category generally applicable in India. For other countries there may be some other statutory compliances and also there may be some other additional statutory compliance depending upon different industry/business requirement.

CONSTITUTION RELATED

Here there is pre-requisite registrations for an organisation before investing in capital is discussed. Every organisation has to follow certain registration to have its business name in place. And after registrations, it needs to fulfil requirement of that registration by providing periodical reports, payment of fees etc. some of that are discussed herewith:

- ✓ Registrar of Companies/ LLP (ROC):
  - ○ Obtaining Certificate of Incorporation / Commencement certificate
  - ○ Registration of Directors (Obtaining DIN, Form DIR-12)
  - ○ Full time CFO / Company Secretary requirement
  - ○ Board meeting / General Meeting compliances

- o Corporate Social Responsibility (CSR) compliances, if applicable.
  - o Annual Final Accounts and Audit (Internal, Cost & Statutory) etc
- ✓ Registrar of Partnership firm in case of partnership, which is relatively easy than ROC.
- ✓ RBI Compliances in case of Foreign Investors (FDI policy)
- ✓ In case of special category of business, such as banking/insurance etc, there may be other rules and regulation, which may require other registrations.

BUSINESS RELATED

Management should ensure what type of licenses needs to be required to carry on business. Such as to start with a business should have trade license/ shop establishment from local municipal authorities, below are some of license listing in case of various business:

- ✓ Trade License – Applicable in case of business in trading / storing of Goods
- ✓ Shop Establishment – Any type of office open in city where trade licence is not applicable
- ✓ FSSAI – in case of organisation deals in any food items.
- ✓ Import-Export Code (IEC) – In case organisation deals in import or export of goods

✓ Custom House Agents (CHA) – In case of organisation provide clearing & forwarding services.
✓ MTO registration – In case of organisation deals in Multi-Model Transport Operations.
✓ Etc.

After Obtaining such licenses organisation needs to follow rules and regulations as per respective laws in relation to Payment of Fees, Renewal, Insurance, Reporting etc.

LABOUR / INDUSTRIAL RELATED

Here Registration with statutory authority and compliance with same is depend upon strength of work force in the organisation. Further some registrations are required even organisation have 1-2 employees. These are discussed as below:

✓ **Labour welfare registration** - with each state in India where organisation has office, where:
  o Contribution to be deposited as per rules of respective state.
  o And return also to be filed as per rules of respective state
✓ **Provident Fund** – If organisation employs 10 or more People, then it is required to have provident fund registration. Provident fund is basically designed to

have retiral benefits to Employees at the time of their retirement or in case of emergencies. where:

- o To register every employee with KYC (UAN)
- o To deposit every month contribution from Salary of each employee by 15th of Following month.
- o Failure to deposit money in time may have penalties in Income Tax
- o To file other returns (such as International worker, working women details etc)

✓ **Employee State Insurance (ESI)**– Similar to PF, ESI is also applicable if organisation employs 10 or more People. ESI is designed to safeguard lower class of employees for medical emergency of their family; where:

- o To register every employee who has total monthly salary up to INR 21,000/-
- o Contribution is 1.75% of employee and 4.75% of employer of total salary.
- o In case of Contract labour also, there should be liability of principal employer to deposit ESI for casual labour charges paid to contractor.
- o To deposit every month contribution from Salary of each employee by 15th of Following month.
- o Failure to deposit money in time may have penalties in Income Tax

✓ **Professional Tax** – Professional tax currently applicable in selected states in India, if organisation has office in those states, then it is required to register with professional tax authorities and:

- o To deduct employee contribution every month from salary and to deposit with authorities as per dues dates
- o To deposit employer contribution with authorities (Its generally Annual)
- o To file return with respective authorities.

DIRECT TAXES (INCOME TAX)

✓ **Advance Income Tax:** As per income tax rules, every person needs to estimate his tax for every financial year and needs to deposit in defined instalment during the year to avoid interests, so it is necessary for organisation to pay **advance tax** on each due date by doing below:

- o Estimation of Profit for the whole year
- o Estimation of Depreciation on fixed assets
- o Estimation of Tax Deducted at source by Parties
- o Estimation of various disallowance or extra allowance
- o Estimation of Tax Liability and instalment amount due
- o Pay Tax by Challan 280
- o Failure to pay advance tax more than INR 10,000/- liable for interest @1% per month or

part thereof. Which is effectively about 17% p.a. against bank loan interest.

- o Income tax return along with all audit report and CA certificates needs to be submitted on or below:
    - For individual/HUF not requiring audit – 31st Jul
    - For other person but requiring Transfer pricing audit – 30th Nov
    - For other persons – 30th Sep

✓ **Tax Deducted at Source (TDS)**

As per Income tax rules, when a business / person thereof pays expenses to vendors/ employees, there is need to deduct a defined portion from payment to payee and deposit the same with government, along with Payee Information in periodical returns, it is termed as **Tax Deducted at source (TDS).** Below are key points to note:

- o Deduction of Tax at given rates at the time earlier of payment or credit in books.
- o Section 192 – TDS on salary payment:
    - Estimation of each employee taxable income (Actual + Estimation)
    - Estimation of Deductions
    - Estimation of Tax Liability
    - TDS for the month

- [(Est Tax Liability – TDS deducted till previous month)/Balance no. of months in FY]
  o Section 194A – Tax @10% on payment of interest to party other than banks/financial institution in excess of INR 5000 in a FY.
  o Section 194B/BB – Tax @30% on Payment of lottery, game prizes, horse races etc in excess of INR 10000 in a FY.
  o Section 194C – Tax @ 1% to Individual / HUF and 2% to Firms/ Association/Companies/ others on payment of any contract fee in excess of INR 100000 in a FY or INR 30000 for an invoice.
  o Section 194H – Tax @5% on commission paid to any person in excess of INR 15,000 in a F.Y.
  o Section 194I-A – Tax @2% on rent of machinery or equipment to any person in cases of INR 180000/- in FY.
  o Section 194I-B – Tax @10% on rent of Building/ Furniture and fittings etc in excess of INR 180000/- in a FY
  o Section 194J – Tax @10% on Professional / Royalty/ Technical Fee to any person in excess of INR 30000/- in a FY. Also 10% TDS is applicable on any director remuneration.
  o Section 195 -Tax on payments to Non-Residents (Foreigners) @ Rates in force (Income Tax Act) or as per Double Taxation Avoidance Agreement (DTAA), if Applicable.

- o Section 197 – TDS @ lower rates in case any person obtain permission from income tax for such rate basis his financial vs Tax due from him.
- o Section 206AA- in case of non-availability of PAN of vendor, TDS to be deducted @ 20%.
- o There certain exemption or relaxed rates for certain class of payments/persons.
- o Payment of Tax by 7th of Following month for each month except Mar, where Due date is 30th April for payment of tax.
- o Submission of quarterly Return of TDS deduction and deposit along with all details, like, Pan, Amount, deduction Date, Payment date etc. Due date is One month following end of quarter except for mar where its 31st May.
- o Issuance of TDS certificate (form 16/16A) to deductees by 15th day following due date of TDS return.

✓ **Tax Collected at Source (TCS)**
  - o This tax is collected / recovered from buyer at the time of sale of some specified goods, majorly scrap, Forest produce, bullion exceeding INR 2 Lacs, Jewellery exceeding INR 5 Lacs etc.
  - o It's generally 1% of sale value, and for some cases it is up to 5%.
  - o There is certain class of persons who exempt from this such as a person who is not liable for Tax Audit etc.

- o Tax collected to be deposited by 7th of following month.
- o Return for tax collected needs to be submitted by 15th day following end of quarter.
- o Likewise, TDS certificate, TCS certificate is also issued within 15 days following due date to submit quarterly return, and called form 27D.
- o TCS is also starting in GST for e-commerce operators from 1st Oct 2018 for almost all class of goods.

✓ **Tax Audit (Section 44AB)**

- o Applicable to every person having sale of more than INR 10 Mn /gross receipt in profession more than INR 5 Mn
- o Also applicable to certain class of person if they show less income as percentage to their turnover. (section 44BB, 44AD, 44AE etc.)
- o Tax Audit to be completed by 30th Sep following end of Each financial year on 31st March.
- o Tax Audit is to be done by a chartered accountant in practice.
- o In case, where transfer pricing audit is also required, tax audit due date is relaxed up to 30th Nov.
- o Transfer pricing audit is required if any person has any international transaction with its foreign related party or domestic transactions more than a certain limit with local related parties.

✓ **Gift** received in excess of INR 50,000 also taxable in hands of person except some certain cases. And Income tax at normal rates is due.

INDIRECT TAXES

✓ **Custom Duty**
- o Payable of duties at the time of import of goods in India
- o There is requirement to file documents for goods arrival in 1 day
- o Failure to same, penalty becomes payable.
- o There is huge list of items specify various duty rates for different items.
- o Duty to be paid within 1 day of assessment of documents otherwise interest is payable @15% per annum.
- o Custom department keeps eye on prices of goods, whether undervalued or overvalued.
- o In case of Undervalued items or goods from some specified countries, it added assessable value/additional duty and in case overvalued items, case is being referred to special investigation team doubting case of money laundering.
- o Presently, Custom duty generally has below structure:
    - ▪ Basic Custom Duty
    - ▪ Any Additional Duty, if applicable

- IGST on Assessable value + Basic Custom duty + Additional Duty.
- o Below link provided by custom department to know custom duty amount on particular type of goods:

  https://www.icegate.gov.in/Webappl/index_imp.jsp

- o Custom allows duty drawback or incentive scheme also if organisation has exports also subjected to certain rules and regulations.

✓ **Excise Duty:**
- o Presently excise duty is almost abolished after implementation of GST since Jul 2017. However, it is still there for petroleum and tobacco products. But not discussed here since it is not applicable for mostly organisations.

✓ **Goods and Service Tax (GST)**
- o Since 1st Jul 2017, GST is implemented after merging Excise Duty, Service Tax, Central Sales Tax (CST, Local Value added tax (VAT), and other local state taxes.
- o Every person needs to have GST registration with each state, where he having office.
- o GST is segregated in IGST (Inter-state GST), CGST (Central GST) and SGST/UGST (State / Union Territory GST).

- o Place of Supply (POS) is key factor in determining whether IGST is applicable or CGST and SGST/UGST is applicable. POS is state where goods/services are rendered.
- o POS generally is place of registered buyer. However, in certain cases it differs. If POS is same state as of Seller, then CGST and SGST/UGST is applicable otherwise IGST.
- o GST collected from customers against sales needs to be deposited with government after adjusting input GST paid on purchases to registered buyers subjected to defined rules.
- o In some cases, GST is to be paid on specified purchases as well, like Imports, Lawyer services etc.
- o GST input can be taken within 1 year from date of invoice or Sep month following end of financial year for which invoice pertains, whichever is earlier.
- o For small business man, there are some relaxation in GST, such as exemption for business having Turnover less than INR 2 Mn, Composition option to pay tax at specified nominal rates and to have simple compliance, quarterly return submission instead monthly etc.
- o There are different rules for export of goods / services for Bond or letter of undertaking for not paying IGST on exports. Also, for refund of IGST

paid on exports or GST paid on purchases used in exports.

- o There are various returns which needs to be submitted at online portal, where majorly are below:
  - GSTR 1 – Return for Sales (generally due on 10th of following month)
  - GSTR 2 – Return for Purchases (generally due on 15th of following month - presently waived)
  - GSTR 3 – Summary of Sales, Purchases and Payment. (presently summarised form naming GSTR 3B is applicable and due on 20th of following month).
- o There may be other certain rules specific to business requirement.

*****

Key Documents – Tax Calendar / Compliance Chart.

RISK MANAGEMENT

Risk management requirement has been increased in today scenario, wherein risk manager, also known as compliance officer, needs to ensure minimum risk to the organisation in each type of activity, whether pertaining to storing of goods, handling of cash, assets etc. Generally, risk cannot be avoided in business, but it surely be minimised/mitigated by having some third-party contracts, insurance etc and can be described below for each business area:

- ✓ **SALES:** Risk can be minimised by:
  - o Having standard form of sale contract/order/agreement/invoice capturing terms & conditions as per business requirement.
  - o Having defined term and conditions to define ownership

- ✓ **PURCHASES:** Risk can be minimised by:
  - o Having proper procedure in place for various type of purchases based on quantum of purchase, such as Minimum quotation, Quality checks, vendor verification etc.
  - o Proper transfer of Ownership of goods to ensure insurance coverage in transit.
  - o In case of imports, compliance checklist and Insurance coverage

- ✓ **ASSET MANAGEMENT:** Risk can be minimised by:

- o Taking AMC of various Assets, such as security devices, IT Devices, Mechanical Devices and other electronic devices
- o Taking Cash Fidelity insurance for handling cash in terms of holding/Carrying etc.
- o Taking Inventory insurance if applicable.
- o Taking Marine insurance for goods in transit till point of ownership with organisation. i.e., till delivery for sales / from delivery for purchases
- o Taking Insurance of Various other Assets. (office floater insurance policy is more popular for this, which covers Building, Furniture, Cash Fidelity, All risk, mechanical breakdown, electrical failure, inventory/warehousing etc)

RISK MITIGATION BY INTERNAL AUDIT:

Internal audit is also a tool for mitigating risk in the organisation. Generally internal audit is mandatory for certain class of organisations; however, it is advisable to have inhouse or outsourced internal audit team with commensurate with size of organisation.

Internal Audit is generally on quarterly basis and covers various aspects of controls and produce reports showing gaps in controls or areas of improvement to the management, by which organisation can minimize gaps in controls or improve business efficiency, and same ultimately results in reduction in Risk of loss/less profit in business, wrong-doing, inefficiency of manpower etc.

Internal audit covers various areas including below:

- ✓ Correct and Timely Billing
- ✓ Timely and controlled Procurement
- ✓ Cost Reduction and Controlling
- ✓ Statutory Compliance
- ✓ Contracts/agreement management
- ✓ Manpower management
- ✓ Corporate Governance
- ✓ Risk Analysis and reporting
- ✓ Technological controls (Information system / ERP)
- ✓ Etc.

*****

Key Documents – Process Flows (SOPs) for Purchase / Sales / Audit etc.

PRICING / RELEVANT & ABSORPTION COSTING

(A GUIDANCE TO SALES)

Before proceeding with method to establishing sales pricing, we need to discuss some of the key factors / cost elements, as below:

✓ **Fixed Cost** – It's a cost which is fixed in nature and does not depend on quantum of sales to a sizable extent, such as Office rent, Staff cost, Office expenses, Fixed Assets depreciation etc.

✓ **Variable Cost** – It's a cost which is varied upon quantum of sales, such as Direct Material, Direct Service cost (outsourced) for sales, Labour cost etc.

✓ **Semi – Fixed / Variable Cost** – These costs are in fixed in nature and varied after a quantum of sales. E.g. in a service organization, an operation staff can handle 20 sales service tasks in a day, and if sales tasks increased to 30-35, these is need of additional staff, that cost becomes semi – variable.

✓ **Absorption costing** – Absorption costing is a method to allocate against each sales unit, so that profitability can be analysed for each sales unit, customer, branch, segment etc. Variable cost can be allocated directly to sales unit identified, the matter comes here to allocate fixed cost, also called as overhead. There are generally two ways to allocate cost such as;
  o **Traditional Absorption** – in this, cost is allocated based on One Popular Base useful for

organisation, e.g. no. of units, hour consumed for produced/sales unit etc.

- o **Activity Based costing** – In this cost is first divided into various activities and for each activity different base is used as per business use. E.g. while distributing cost in segment, office rent is divided basis no. of employees in each segment, Assets depreciation is divided in ratio of investment in each segment and so on. And this is better way to allocate cost in comparison to traditional absorption.

✓ **Relevant Cost** – It's in general a variable cost which is relevant to any decision making. Its importance comes into picture when a decision to be taken for accepting or rejecting. And for taking decision, all relevant costs including opportunity cost are being considered while no past costs, Called Sunk Costs are considered.

✓ **Opportunity cost** – It's a cost of forgoing profit on alternative decision. E.g. if a company earns a return of 7% on its excess funds and if company use this money in other investment, a cost of 7% return forgoing in investment is a cost to other investment.

Now above elements can be used to determine how pricing to be built for sales. There are generally two ways:

✓ **Cost Plus Method:** in this, organization analysis its cost at each unit basis and then arrive to sale price after adding desired margin. It's a traditional way but presently this method is used after analysing more such as below:

- o **In start-up:** In start-up business, overheads are more and if all overhead allocated to sales unit and then using cost plus method sale price will not be competitive, and for meeting this, organisation should analysis first contribution desired on each sales unit, where:

Contribution = Sales price less Variable / Relevant Cost

Then this contribution to be compared with Fixed costs, and the to arrive approachable Break-even point, where All cost can be recovered from sales. If this break-even point can be approached in desired period, then contribution basis can be considered, i.e., to recover variable costs first from sales.

This method also used in case, where fixed cost is not related to decision acceptance/rejection or sales a X quantity or Y quantity. And management can be able to decide whether to accept proposal of sales if contribution is positive and no relation to fixed cost.

E.g. in case of start-up business, a customer in different region ask for sales at X price, and the same is outsourced to third party, at 95% of X, if taking no other relevant factor, contribution/margin @5% will be better or organization as no resource is being used in this.

o **In Successful Running business** – In case of running business, overheads are mitigated over a period of time, and actual cost at each unit can be arrived by using either traditional absorbing or activity based absorbing costing. And a desired margin added to cost will give desired sales price.

Sale price = Variable Cost + Overhead allocated to sales

✓ **Reference Price / Market Price -** This is another way to decide pricing of sales, where cost is not preferred in decision to arrive price rather price available in market is being preferred such as competitor price, government regulated price etc.

However, while using this method, a care needs to be taken on impact of sales on organisation in terms of profitability. Because in some cases reference price could give negative / less margin to the organisation, and organisation cannot sustain the same in long run for same depending upon other factors.

E.g., a factory established in ruler area can have lower labour cost in comparison to factory in urban area. And if labour cost is more in product cost, an urban factory cannot sustain sales prices as for ruler factory due to cost mismatch. So, organisation needs to decide, where to shift factory or to go for alternative product to sustain business.

For keeping eye on the reference price, profitability can be presented to management on monthly basis showing:

Sales - Direct Costs = Contribution - Overhead allocation cost = Profit / (loss)

And the same can be presented at sales unit level, group / segment level, branch level, and at organisation as whole level.

*****

Key Documents – Process Flows (SOPs) for overhead allocation and profitability format.

F&A MANPOWER MANAGEMENT

In every organisation, it is required to have manpower in F&A department as commensurate to size of business. In Running business, it is easy to have a definite number of manpower as per need of business, however in start-up or growing business, it is difficult to decide manpower exactly in line with size of business.

So, to get away from this difficulty, F&A head needs to detailed all job description at activity level, then to cumulate certain activities to arrive a job description for a particular staff. If that is done, it will be easy to decide manpower planning.

Detailing of Job Description can be done by putting data in below Table:

Sr. No.	Branch/ Segment	Activity	Quantum	Periodicity	Time Required (Minutes)	Monthly Hours (Q * P * M /60)
1	XX	Billing	3000	Monthly	8	400 (3000*1*8/60)

In above example, billing need 400 men hours in a month. And if office hours for each employee is 25*8 = 200 hours in a month, it can show requirement of 2 Persons for billing only and so on.

This method is also effective if in a developed / running organisation, there is need to re-plan manpower after restructuring/ New ERP implementation etc.

E.g. If taking above table example, company decide to implement CRM (Customer Relation Management Software) or new ERP system, where sales/ops team puts billing data / sales order and by same, time required for billing person reduced to 4 min instead 8 minutes for each bill, and by using this method of Manpower Analysis, there will be Total reduction of manhours to monthly 200 from 400 and accordingly it can be decided by management to reduce 1 manpower from billing and to use that resource at other place.

F&A functions is already discussed in this whole document before and accordingly job description and manpower can be planned.

*****

Key Documents – F&A Team Job Description Detailing and summary thereof

USE OF INFORMATION TECHNOLOGY (IT) TOOLS

In present days, IT has vast role in day-to-day routine in every business and in each functional area, to have:

✓ Better Reporting with useful information at tips
✓ Increased Efficiency of Staff
✓ Minimum errors
✓ Time Saving
✓ Minimum Manpower Dependency
✓ Easy Compliance

Some of IT related tips are as follows:

✓ Use of Good Accounting Software / package as per business requirement
✓ Use of Good Operation software (if not opted for ERP or integrated ops & Accounts software)
✓ Controlling Integration of Softwares used in one organisation (If more than 1)
✓ Maintaining of Data in Soft form
✓ Use of Online Drive
✓ Periodic Data Backup policies.
✓ Use of MS excel in best form (a tool for Smart Accountant) (Imparting training)
✓ Automation of various reports to possible extent, such as:
    o Sales report
    o Debtors / Creditors Report
    o Bank Reconciliation statement (Presently many accounting softwares provide auto BRS where

almost 80-85% reconciliation is done by software itself)

- o Manpower Attendance / leaves/ Payroll etc.
- o Efficiency reports
- ✓ Use of Tax Softwares to have easy compliance
- ✓ Etc.

*****

Key Documents – Listing of Possible IT solution for Organisation

CONCLUSION / SUMMARIZATION

We have discussed about F&A functions and F&A need/support required in organisation in other functional level. we have detailed requirement of F&A function in almost each business process area involve in organisation, whether for debtor, creditors, banking, compliance, assets, sales, purchase or any other area.

As we have given key documentation requirement for each F&A area herein, and same is being summarized herein below to know which are major documents and formats generally needed in an organisation to have better control of finance and accounting (Compiling of which can be called as Accounting and Finance manual / SOP for the organisation):

- ✓ Policy / Procedures (SOPs):
    - o Customer / Credit Management Policy
    - o Delegation of Authority (DOA) Policy
    - o Process Flows (SOPs) for:
        - Purchase
        - Sales (including pre-billing, billing, Bill submission)
        - Audit
        - Overhead allocation at Unit level
        - Payment (Disbursement Checklist)
- ✓ Tax Calendar / Compliance Chart

- ✓ Control sheet Renewal dates due for contracts, agreement, Licenses etc.
- ✓ Report Format and Other documents' standardisation:
  - o Annual Budget Formats
  - o MIS Formats
  - o Debtors Reports Formats
  - o Accounts Payable Report Format
  - o Unit Level Profitability Report format
  - o No Dues letter format
  - o PDC Letter Format
  - o BRS Format
  - o Funds Flows Report Format
  - o Invoice Format
- ✓ F&A Team Job Description Detailing and summary thereof
- ✓ Listing of Possible IT solution for Organisation
- ✓ Any other data as per business requirement

****